On the Moon

With thanks to Stuart Atkinson for information about the Moon missions
Managing Editor: Gillian Doherty
Photographs © NASA; photographs of Earth © Digital Vision

On the Moon

Anna Milbourne

Illustrated by Benji Davies

Designed by Laura Fearn

The Moon is very,
very far away.

What do you think it
would be like to go there?

A few people have been to the Moon.
Astronauts went there to see what it was like.

If you went to the Moon
you'd be an astronaut too.

To get to the Moon, you have to go in a huge rocket.

Five...

four...

three...

two...

one...

Lift off!

The astronauts sit in a tiny cabin at the very top.

The rocket flies into space.

There's nothing but stars
and darkness all around.

It takes four whole days to reach the Moon.

When you get there,
you climb into a
little spaceship.

It flies down...

and down...

and lands gently on the Moon.

To go outside, you have to put on a space suit.

There is no air on the Moon.
Space suits carry air so you can breathe.

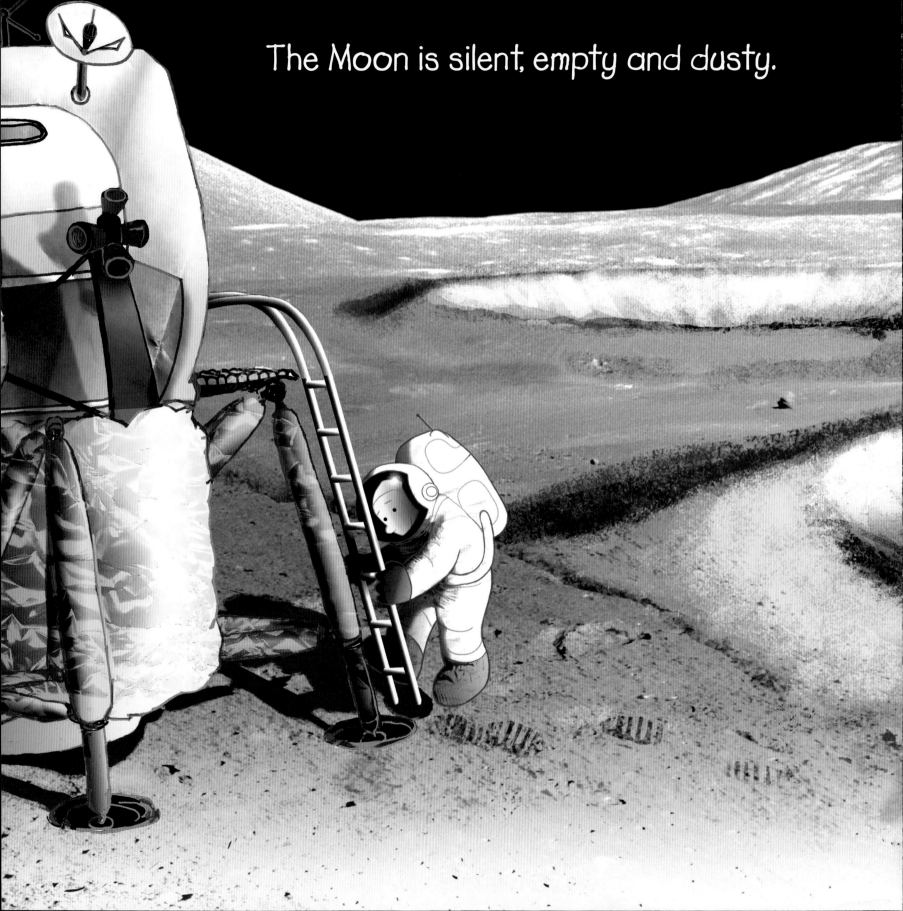

The Moon is silent, empty and dusty.

There are huge mountains...

and big holes.

But there are no trees or
water, no animals or people.

On the Moon, you feel very light and floaty.

When you walk around,
you take big, bouncing strides.

You can jump really far –
much further than you can at home.

Astronauts sometimes go exploring in Moon buggies.

They collect Moon rocks to bring back home.

They take photos to show people
at home what the Moon looks like.

Astronauts put a flag on the Moon to show they have been there.

You can see our world from the Moon.

It looks tiny because it is so far away.

When it's time to go, the
astronauts blast off for home.

The Moon is left almost as it was before,

apart from a flag and a buggy

and some footprints in the dust.

Do you think you'll ever go to the Moon?